Angels

To: _____

From: _____

Designed by Roni Akmon
Edited by Nancy Cogan Akmon

Blushing Rose Publishing
San Anselmo, California

*J*acob dreamed there was a
    ladder set up on the earth; and
the top of it reached to heaven;
and behold the angels of God were
ascending and descending upon it.
                    Genesis 28:12

*B*less the Lord, Ye his angels, mighty ones who do his commands, harkening unto the voice of his words.

Psalms 103:20

I Dreamt a Dream! what can it mean?
And that I was a maiden Queen:
Guarded by an Angel mild:
Witless woe, was neer beguil'd!

And I wept both night and day
And he wip'd my tears away
And I wept both day and night
And hid from him my hearts delight

So he took his wings and fled:
Then the morn blush'd rosy red:
I dried my tears & armd my fears,
With ten thousand shields and spears.

Soon my Angel came again:
I was arm'd, he came in vain:
For the time of youth was fled
And grey hairs were on my head

William Blake

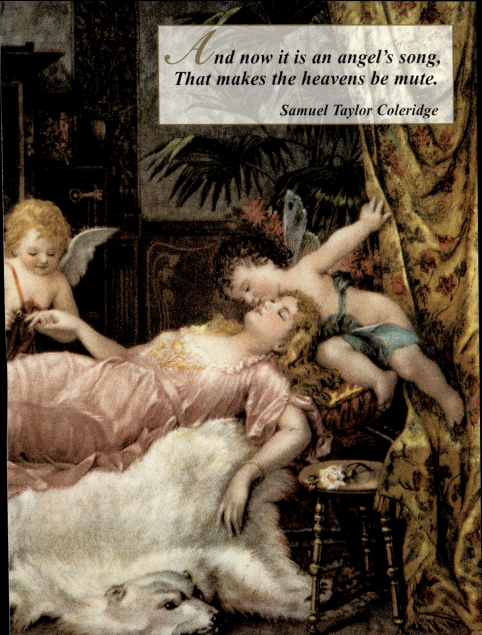

*A*nd now it is an angel's song,
That makes the heavens be mute.

Samuel Taylor Coleridge

The angel of the flowers one day
beneath a Rose-tree Sleeping lay
Awaking from his light response,
the Angel whispered to the Rose,
fondest object of my care,
still fairest found where all is fair
For the sweet shade thou give to me,
ask what thou wilt 'tis granted thee.
Then said the Rose with deepened glory,
on me another grace bestow.
The spirit paused in silent thought.
What grace was the flower had not?
Twas but a moment—over the Rose a
veil of moss the Angel throws,
And robed in nature's simplest weed, could
there a flower that Rose exceed?

Thou fair-haired angel of the evening,
Now, whilst the sun rests on the mountains, light
Thy bright torch of love; thy radiant crown
Put on, and smile upon our evening bed!
Smile on our loves, and, while thou drawest the
Blue curtains of the sky, scatter thy silver dew
On every flower that shuts its sweet eyes
In timely sleep. Let thy west wind sleep on
The lake; speak silence with thy glimmering eyes,
And wash the dusk with silver. Soon, full soon,
Dost thou withdraw; then the wolf rages wide,
And the lion glares through the dun forest:
The fleeces of our flocks are covered with
Thy sacred dew: protect them with thine influence.

William Blake

I looked over Jordan and
what did I see?
Comin' for to carry me home
A band of angels comin' after me,
Comin' for to carry me home.

Swing Low,
Sweet Chariot

No evil shall befall you,
No plague come near your tent;
For he shall give his angels charge of
you to guard you in all your ways.
On their hands they will bear you up
lest you dash your foot against a stone.

Psalms 91:10,11,12

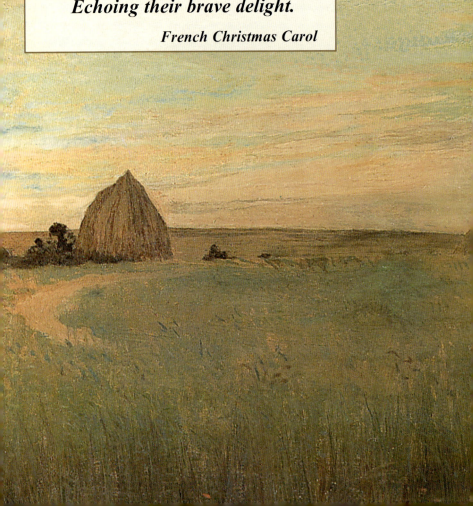

*A*ngels,we have heard on high
Singing sweetly through the night,
And the mountains in reply
Echoing their brave delight.

French Christmas Carol

*F*or He shall give His angels charge over thee, to keep thee in all thy ways.

Psalms 91:2

Good night sweet prince,
And flights of angels sing thee
to thy rest.

Shakespeare